T0374260

The CELEBRATION of Life

The CELEBRATION of Life

REV. FR. DR. ALPHONSUS E. OBI

THE CELEBRATION OF LIFE

Copyright © 2024 Rev. Fr. Dr. Alphonsus E. Obi.

All rights reserved. No part of this book may be used or reproduced by any means, graphic, electronic, or mechanical, including photocopying, recording, taping or by any information storage retrieval system without the written permission of the author except in the case of brief quotations embodied in critical articles and reviews.

iUniverse books may be ordered through booksellers or by contacting:

iUniverse
1663 Liberty Drive
Bloomington, IN 47403
www.iuniverse.com
844-349-9409

Because of the dynamic nature of the Internet, any web addresses or links contained in this book may have changed since publication and may no longer be valid. The views expressed in this work are solely those of the author and do not necessarily reflect the views of the publisher, and the publisher hereby disclaims any responsibility for them.

Any people depicted in stock imagery provided by Getty Images are models, and such images are being used for illustrative purposes only. Certain stock imagery © Getty Images.

ISBN: 978-1-6632-4023-1 (sc)
ISBN: 978-1-6632-4024-8 (e)

Library of Congress Control Number: 2024900090

Print information available on the last page.

iUniverse rev. date: 04/03/2024

CONTENTS

"The Celebration Of Life, Wake Or Wake-Keeping"

Why celebration of Life? It is called celebration of life in recognition of a departed member of our community and all the children of God in this world who left this world to join the creator in Heaven. Whether it is called wake or wake-keeping all gears towards the provision of a service prior to burial in a social gathering. Traditionally, this is done at the home of the deceased with the body present. Recently wakes are often performed at a funeral home or at a hall preferably chosen by the members of the deceased family. It is often a social rite which highlights the fact that the loss affects the whole group. The term "wake" originally referred to a late-night prayer vigil, which is mostly used for the social interaction. While this modern usage of the verb "wake" means to stay alert. A wake for the dead harks back to the vigil, "watch" or "guard" of earlier times. It is a misconception that people at wake are waiting in case the deceased should wake up. The term "wake" originated from the Middle English "waken". Waken, from the old English, "wacan" means to wake up and, "wacian" means to be awake and to keep watch. This was originally meant to denote a prayer vigil, often used as an annual event held in honor of the feast day of a saint or saints to whom a church was dedicated, such as St. Paul, St John, St Augustine, St Lucy, St Mary etc. in the rural areas of the world before embalming was practiced, people would try or like to wake the body. The custom was to sit with deceased constantly, usually for two nights to make sure the person in question was truly dead.

In summary wake-keep or wake keeping is organized by the survivors of the deceased to basically raise fund for the burial rite. Wake-keep or wake keeping as commonly used, which means to keep vigil over a corpse the night before the burial, usually associated with prayer, singing gospel songs, songs of praise and other songs etc. on the other hand, celebration of life could be used for those who are alive. We can celebrate when we return to God from our sinful way of life; accept that we have offended God in many ways and make a U turn to God when we then realize that God the merciful father has forgiven us, we can celebrate, having come back to God the creator, make amendments of our lives. So this book "Celebration of life is for those who are dead and those who are living.

The introduction of this book on page 4 and 5 will tell us more about our relationship with God and ourselves.

DEDICATION

These pamphlets have been dedicated to all people of God, made in His own image and likeness, especially those who have died, gone before us marked with the sign of faith.

INTRODUCTION

I was motivated to write these pamphlets together especially at any wake-keep when I share any of these pamphlets with people of God, and at the end of each wake-keep, when I demand back the copies shared out to people to returned them to me, I notice that the reaction of few individuals is disappointment, because they thought they were supposed to keep the pamphlets permanently hence the publication of these piece to eliminate that disappointment people get when they are asked to return the pamphlets. Some persons even went as far as asking for the price to get a copy, so that they can get a copy. The wake helps us to reflect more on ourselves, to think seriously about our relationship with God, and our neighbors. In St. Mark chapter 12 vs 29 – 31, a teacher of law asked Jesus which commandment is the first? And Jesus answered, "The first is: Hear, Israel, the Lord, our God is one Lord, and you shall love the Lord your God with all your heart, with all your soul, with your entire mind and with all your strength. And after this comes another one, you shall love your neighbor as yourself. There is no commandment greater than these two" We need to ask ourselves, why God made us and what is our duty as children of God? What is required in our journey here on earth and what will the end of our time be like? Recall the beautiful song, "This world is not my home I'm just a passing through, my treasures are laid up somewhere beyond the blue; the angels beckon me from heaven's open door, and can't feel at home in this world anymore.

CHORUS

O Lord, you know I have no friend like you, if heaven's not my home, then Lord what will do? The angels beckon me from heaven's open door, and I can't feel at home in this world anymore. God our Father is very patient and merciful; He has given us the opportunity to know and serve him in this world and do all that is required of us as special children of God and be with Him at the end of our time in Heaven. This needs a total surrender of oneself to God. Remember the words of our Lord Jesus Christ in St. Matthew's gospel chapter 11:28 "come to me all who labor and are burdened and I will refresh you". Remember also same St. Matthew: Chapter 10:33 "whoever rejects me before others, I will reject before my Father in Heaven". Once more, let these pamphlets remind us that our journey here on earth is just for a little time, and that this world will soon pass, and there is a place we are aiming to go that will never have an end. These pamphlets are asking us very big questions: ARE WE READY"? ARE WE PREPARED FOR IT"? These pamphlets are good for everybody. The content will help us reflect on ourselves, and our purpose on earth. May the Almighty God bless and keep us safe always, through Jesus Christ Our Lord. Amen!

Chapter 1

PAMPHLET A

ORDER OF SERVICE:
LEADER:
THE OPENING PRAYER!

Let us pray,

Oh! God our father, who willed that your only Begotten Son Jesus Christ, having conquered death, should pass over into the realm of Heaven, grant as we pray for your departed servant (Name of the deceased.........)

That with the mortality of this life overcome he/she may gaze eternally on you his/her Creator and Redeemer, through Jesus Christ our Lord. Amen.

(Please all continue standing).

OPENING HYMN
ABIDE WITH ME:

1. Abide with me; fast falls the eventide,
    The darkness deepens; Lord with me abide,
    When others helpless fall and comforts flee,
    Help of the helpless, O" abide with me.

2. Swift to its close ebbs out life's little day,
    Earth's joy grows dim its glories pass away,
    Change and decay in all around I see;
    O" Thou who changest not, abide with me

3. I need Thy presence every passing hour,
    What but Thy grace can foll the tempter's power?
    Who, like thyself, my guide and stay can be?
    Through clouds and sunshine, Lord, abide with me.

4. I fear no for, with Thee at hand to bless;
    Ills have no weight, and tear no bitterness,
    Where is death's sting? Where grave, thy victory?
    I triumph still, if Thou abide with me.

5. Hold Thou cross before my closing eyes;
    Shine through the gloom and points me to the skies
    Heaven's morning breaks and earth's vain shadows flee;
    In life, in death, O" Lord abide with me.

FIRST READING: (ALL SIT PLEASE).

A reading from the book of Ecclesiastes (anybody may be appointed by the priest/Leader to read, especially from the deceased family.) Ecclesiastes Chapter 1:2, 2:21-23.

"VANITY OF VANITY ALL ARE VANITY"

Vanity of vanity, the preacher says, vanity of vanities, all is vanity. For so it is that a man who labored wisely, skillfully and successfully must leave what is his own to someone who has not toiled for it all. This too, is vanity and injustice, for what does he gain for all the toil and strain that he has undergone under the sun? What of all his laborious days, his cares of office, his restless nights? This too, is vanity. This is the word of the Lord. All: Thanks, be to God.

RESPONSORIAL PSALM:

Psalm 23. (Could be read or sang by the first reader or anyone from the audience).

(All stand please).

THE RESPONSE IS:

A.) My Shepherd is the Lord, nothing indeed shall I want.
B.) The Lord is my shepherd; there is nothing I shall want.
C.) His goodness shall follow me always, till the end of my days

1. The Lord is my shepherd: there is nothing I shall want,
   Fresh and green are the pastures,
   Where he gives me repose,
   Near restful waters he leads me;
   To revive my drooping spirit.

Response:

2. He guides me along the right part,
   He is true to his name
   If I should walk in the valley of darkness
   No evil would I fear
   You are there with your crook and your staff
   With these you give me comfort.

Response:

3. You have prepared a banquet for me,
   In the sight of my foes,
   My head you have anointed with oil,
   My cup is overflowing.

Response:

4. Surely goodness and kindness shall follow me,
    All the days of my life,
    In the Lord's own house shall I dwell,
    Forever and ever.

Response:

SECOND READING: LEADER COULD APPOINT ANYBODY TO READ ESPECIALLY ANY MEMBER FROM THE DECEASED FAMILY)

A reading from the book of St. Paul to the Corinthians,

1st Corinthians Chapter 15:21-27.

A man brought death; a man also brings resurrection of the dead.

All die for being Adam's; and in Christ all will receive life, however, each one in his own time; first Christ, then Christ's people when he visits them.

Then the end will come, when Christ delivers the kingdom to God the Father, after having destroyed every rule, authority and power.

For he must reign and put all enemies under his feet. The last enemy to be destroyed will be death.

As Scripture says: God has subjected everything under His feet.

The Word of the Lord.

All: Thanks, be to God.

GOSPEL ACCLAMATION:

(All please stand, sing or read)
Alleluia! Alleluia!! I am the resurrection and life;
Whoever believes in me though he dies?
Shall live forever
Alleluia!

LEADER:

(All please continue to stand)
The Gospel of our Lord Jesus Christ according to St. Luke
Chapter 12:35-47.

ALL: GLORY TO YOU O LORD

Be ready dressed for service, and keep your lamps lit, like people waiting for their master to return from the weeding. As soon as he comes and knocks, they will open for him. Happy are those servants whom he finds wide awake when he comes. Truly, I tell you, he will wait on them. Happy are those servants if he finds them awake when he comes at midnight or daybreak. Pay attention to this; If the master of the house had known at what time the thief would come, he would not have let him break into his house. You also must be ready, for the son of man will come at an hour you do not expect. Peter said, Lord, did you tell this parable only for us, or for everyone? And the Lord replied; imagine, then, the wise and the faithful steward whom the master sets over his other servants to give them food rations at the proper time. How fortunate to this servant, if his master on coming home finds him doing his work. Truly, I say to you, the master will put him in charge of all his property. But it may be that the steward thinks: My Lord delays in coming, and he begins to abuse the men servants and the servant girls, eating and drinking and getting drunk. Then the master may come on a day he does not expect him and at an hour he doesn't know. He will discharge his servant and number him among the unreliable. The servant who knew his master's will but did not prepare to do what his master wanted, will be punished with sound blows, but the one who did what deserved a punishment without knowing it shall receive fewer blows. Much will be required of the one who has been given much, and more will be asked of the one entrusted with more.

The Gospel of the Lord.

All: Praise be to you Lord Jesus Christ.
***A short reflection follows from the Scripture readings by the Priest/Leader.

(All please sit.)

INTERCESSIONS: (ALL PLEASE STAND)

PRIEST/LEADER

Let us pray that God our Father will bless us and console us, as we now remember our departed beloved ones who have gone before us marked with the sign of faith especially (Name............of the deceased).

That God our Father who raised Jesus from the dead will give us life to our own mortal bodies as we pray.

All: Lord brings us life in Christ.

LEADER

Holy Father, we have been buried with your Son Jesus in Baptism; to rise with Him in Glory, may we always live in Christ and not to see death as forever.

All: Lord brings us life in Christ.

LEADER

Holy Father, you have given us living bread from Heaven, to be eaten with faith and love, grant that we may have eternal life and be raised up on the last day.

All: Lord brings us life in Christ.

Holy Father, when your son Jesus was in agony, you sent an Angel to console Him, at the hour of our death take away all fear and fill our hearts with hope.

All: Lord brings us life in Christ.

LEADER

Holy Father, you delivered the three young men from the blazing furnace, free the souls of the dead from their sins deserved.

All: Lord brings us life in Christ.

LEADER:

God of the living and the dead,
You brought Jesus back to life,
Raise up your faithful departed especially (Name............ of the deceased.)
And let us come with him/her into your Heavenly Glory.

All: Lord brings us life in Christ.

The Lord's Prayer:
Our Father who at in Heaven,
Hallow be thy name
Thy kingdom come,
Thy will be done
On earth as it is in Heaven

Give us this day our daily bread,
And forgive us our trespasses,
As we forgive those who trespass against us;
And lead us not into temptation,
But deliver us from evil, Amen.

CONCLUDING PRAYERS:

O! God our Father, by whose Son's death and resurrection we have been redeemed,

You are the Glory of Your faithful,

The life of your Saints,

Have mercy on your servant (Name........of the deceased), and he/she professed his/her faith in the Mystery of our resurrection, so may he/she gain possession of eternal joy,

We make our prayers through Jesus Christ Our Lord. Amen.

CONCLUDING HYMN:
BLESSED ASSURANCE:

1. Blessed assurance, Jesus is mine,
    Oh, what a foretaste of glory divine!
    Heir of salvation, purchase of God,
    Born of His Spirit, washed in His Blood.
    This is my story, this is my song,
    Praising my Savior all the day long,
    This is my story, this is my song
    Praising my Savior all the day long.

2. Perfect submission, perfect delight,
   Vision of rapture now burst on my sight,
   Angels descending, bring from above,
   Echoes of mercy, whispers of love.
   This is my.................................

3. Perfect submission, all is at rest,
   I in my Savior am happy and blest,
   Watching and waiting, looking above filled with His goodness, lost
   in His love.
   This is my...

Chapter 2

PAMPHLET B

PRIEST/LEADER:
ORDER OF SERVICE:
LEADER.:
THE OPENING PRAYER,

Let us pray,

O God, giver of pardon and loving author of our salvation, grant, we pray you, in your Mercy, we implore you Father to have Mercy on your servant (Name of the deceased..............) who have passed from this World, may he/she attain a share in eternal happiness, through our lord Jesus Christ, your Son, who lives and reigns with you in the unity of the holy spirit one god forever and ever. Amen.

OPENING HYMN;
AMAZING GRACE,

1. Amazing Grace how sweet the sound, that saved a wretch like me,
   I once was lost but now am found,
   Was blind but now I see?

2. "T was Grace that taught my heart to fear and Grace my fears relieve,
   How precious did that Grace appear?
   The hour I first believe

3. When we've been there ten thousand years,
   Bright shining as the sun,
   We've no less days to sing God's praise,
   Then when we first begun.

4. Amazing Grace, how sweet the sounds,
    That saved a wretch like me,
    I once was lost but now am found,
    Was blind but now I see.
    A M E N.

FIRST READING: (ALL SIT PLEASE).

A reading from the book of Wisdom: (anybody may be appointed by the Priest/Leader to read, especially from the deceased family).

Book of Wisdom Chapter: 3:1-7.

"THE JUST WILL LIVE WITH GOD".

The soul of the just are in the hands of God and no torment shall touch them.

In the eyes of the unwise they appear to be dead,

Their going is held as a disaster; it seems that they lose everything by departing from us, but they are in peace.

Though seeming they have been punished, immortality was the soul of their hope. After slight affliction will come great blessing, for God has tried them and found them worthy to be with Him: after testing them as gold in the furnace, He has accepted them as a holocaust. At the time of his coming they will shine like sparks that run in the stubble.

They will govern nations and rule over peoples, and the Lord will be their king forever.

The word of the Lord.

All: thanks be to God.

RESPONSORIAL PSALM:
PSALM 129 (130)

"If you O Lord should mark our guilt, Lord, who would survive"?

1. Out of the depths, I cry to you O lord,
   Lord, hear my voice!
   O let your ears be attentive,
   To the voice of my pleading.
   Response: If you O Lord should...............

2. If you O Lord should mark our guilt,
   Lord, who would survive?
   But with you is found forgiveness,
   For this we revere you.
   Response: If you O Lord should...............

3. My soul is waiting for the Lord,
   I count on his word,
   My soul is longing for the Lord,
   More than watchman for daybreak,
   Let the watchman count on daybreak,
   And Israel on the Lord.
   Response: If you O Lord should...............

4. Because with the Lord there is mercy,
   And fullness of redemption,
   Israel indeed he will redeem,
   From all its iniquity.
   Response: If you o Lord should...............

2ND READING;

A Reading from the book of St. Paul to the Thessalonians,
Chapter 4:13-18.

Brothers we want you not to be mistaken about those who are already asleep, lest you grieve do those who have no hope.

We believe that Jesus died and rose; it will be the same for those who have died in Jesus. God will bring them together with Jesus and for his sake.

By the same word of the Lord we assert this: those of us who are to be alive at the Lord's coming will not go ahead of those who are already asleep

When the command by the archangel's voice is given, the Lord himself will come down from Heaven while the Divine trumpet call is sounding.

Then those who have died in the Lord will rise first; as for us who are still alive, we will be brought along with them in the clouds to meet the lord in the celestial World. And we will be with the Lord forever.

So then comfort one another with those words.

The word of the Lord.

All: Thanks be to God.

GOSPEL ACCLAMATION:

(Please all stand, read or sing).

Alleluia, Alleluia, stay awake! For you do not know when the Son of man will come, Alleluia, Alleluia.

GOSPEL READING:

Leader:

(Please all remain standing).

A reading from the holy Gospel according to St. John, Chapter: 14: 1-6.

All: Glory to you, O Lord.

Jesus said to his disciples: "do not let your hearts be troubled" You have faith in God; have faith also in me.

In my father's house there are many dwelling places.

If there were not, would I have told you that I am going to prepare a place for you? And if I go and prepare a place for you, I will come back again and take you to myself, so that where I am you also may be. Where I am going you know the way. Thomas said to him "Master, we do not know where you are going: how can we know the way?" Jesus said to him, "I am the way and the truth and the life. No one comes to the father except through me."

The Gospel of the Lord.

All: Praise to you, Lord Jesus Christ.

(All: Please sit.)

*** A reflection follows immediately from the scripture readings by the Priest/Leader.

INTERCESSIONS: (ALL PLEASE STAND.)

Leader:

God, the Almighty Father raised Jesus Christ His Son from the dead; with confidence we ask him to save all his people, living and the dead.

For (name of the deceased.............) who in baptism was given the promise of eternal life, that he/she may be raised up on the last day.

We pray to the Lord.

All: Lord hear our prayers.

For our deceased relatives and friends and all who have helped us, that they may have the reward of their goodness.

We pray to the Lord.

All: Lord hear our prayers.

For all those who have fallen asleep in the hope of rising again, that they may see God face to face.

We pray to the Lord.

All: Lord, hear our prayers.

For (name of the deceased).His/her family and friends, may they be consoled in their grief by Jesus who once wept at the death of His friend Lazarus.

We pray to the Lord.

All: Lord, hear our prayers.

CONCLUDING PRAYERS:

Leader:

God, our shelter and our strength, you listen in Love to the cry of your people; hear the prayers we offer for our departed brothers and sisters, cleanse them of their sins and grant them fullness of redemption,

We ask this through Jesus Christ our Lord.

All; Amen.

CONCLUDING HYMN:
ROCK OF AGES:

1. Rock of Ages cleft for me,
   Let me hide myself in thee;
   Let the water and the blood,
   From thy wounded side which flowed,
   Be of sin the double cure;
   Save from wrath and make me pure.

2. Not the labors of my hands
   Can fulfill thy law's commands;
   Could my zeal no respite know,
   Could my tears forever flow;
   All for sin could not atone;
   Thou must save, and thou alone.

3. Nothing in my hand I bring,
   Simply to the cross I cling;
   Naked, come to thee for dress;
   Helpless, look to thee for grace;
   Foul, I to the fountain fly;
   Wash me, Savior, or I die.

4. While I draw this fleeting breath,
   When my eyes shall close in death,
   When I soar to World's unknown,
   See these on thy judgment throne,
   Rock of Ages, cleft for me,
   Let me hide myself in thee.

Chapter 3

PAMPHLET C

ORDER OF SERVICE;
LEADER
THE OPENING PRAYER,

Let us pray,

Merciful God our Father, you willed that our lives here on earth will end one day, a day we do not know, we humbly pray for friend, brother, sister,(name of the deceased...................) who have gone out of this sinful World, that you will forgive him/her every trace of sin he/she may have committed, knowingly or unknowingly, welcome him/her into your everlasting Kingdom, through Jesus Christ our Lord, who lives and reigns with you in the unity of the Holy Spirit, one God forever and ever. Amen.

(Please remain standing).

OPENING HYMN:

I AM THE BREAD OF LIFE:
I am the bread of life,
He who comes to ME shall not hunger
And who believe in me shall not thirst
No one can come to me
Unless the Father beckon

Chorus:

And I will raise you up
And I will raise you up
And I will raise you up on the last day

The bread that I will give
Is My flesh for the life of the world
And if you eat of this bread
You shall live forever
You shall live forever

Chorus:

And I will raise him up.........
I am the resurrection
I am the life
If you believe in me
Even though you die
You shall live forever

Chorus:

And I will raise him up.........
Yes Lord I believe
That you are the Christ
The Son of God
Who has come
Into the world

Chorus:

And I will raise him up....................

FIRST READING: (ALL PLEASE SIT).

Leader could appoint anybody to read especially any member from the deceased family).

A reading from the book of Sirach:
Chapter 3:1-15.

My children, it is your father who speaks, listen to me and follow my advice and so be saved. For the lord established that children should respect their parents; he confirmed the right of the mother over her sons, whoever honors his father will receive joy from his own children and will be heard when he prays. Whoever glorifies his father will have a long life.

Whoever obeys the Lord gives comfort to his mother.

He serves those who brought him to birth as he would serve the Lord.

Honor your father in word and deed so that his blessing may come on you.

For a father's blessing secures the future of his children, but a mother's curse destroys them at their roots.

Do not rejoice at the humiliation of your father because his dishonor is no glory for you.

For a man's glory comes from his father's reputation; a mother who is not respected is a disgrace to her children.

My son, take care of your father in his old age, do not cause him sorrow as long as he lives.

Even if he has lost his mind, have patience; do not be disrespectful to him while you are in full heath.

For kindness done to one's father will never be forgotten, it will serve as reparation for your sins.

In the days of adversity the Lord will remember it to your advantage; for just as ice melt in the heat, so will your sins will melt away. The man who abandons his father is like a blasphemer; he who annoys his mother is caused by the Lord.

The word of the Lord.

All: thanks be to God.

RESPONSORIAL PSALM: PSALM 130 (could be read or sang by the first reader or anybody from the audience).

RESPONSE:

Lord remember me in your Kingdom.

1. Out of the depths I cry to you, O Lord, Lord hear my voice! O let your ear be attentive to the voice of my pleading.
    Response.........................

2. If you, O Lord should mark our guilt, Lord who would survive? But with you is found forgiveness; for this we revere you.
    Response.........................

3. My soul is waiting for the Lord, I count on his word,
    My soul is longing for the Lord, more than watchman for day break.
    Response.........................

4. Because with the Lord, there is mercy and fullness of redemption, Israel indeed he will redeem from all its iniquity.
    Response.........................

2ND READING: (ALL PLEASE SIT).

Leader could appoint anybody to read, especially any member from the decease family.)

A reading from the letter of St. Paul to the Romans:
Chapter 14:7-9, 10-12.

None of us lives for oneself, and no one dies for oneself,

For if we live, we live for the Lord, and if we die, we are the Lord's.

For this is why Christ died and came to life, that he might be Lord of both the dead and the living. Why then do you judge your brother? Or you, why do you look down on your brother?

For we shall stand before the judgment seat of God, for it is written: "As I live says the Lord, every knee shall bend before me, and every tongue shall give praise to God". So then each of us shall give an account of himself to God.

This is the word of the Lord.

All: Thanks be to God.

GOSPEL ACCLAMATION;

(All please stand, sing or read)

Alleluia, Alleluia,

God so loved the World that he gave His only Son,

Everyone who believes in Him has eternal life.

Alleluia Alleluia.

THE GOSPEL: (All please stand).

Leader:

The gospel of our Lord Jesus Christ according to St. Matthew; Chapter: 25:1-13.

"The Kingdom of heaven will be like ten virgins who took their lamps and went out to meet the bridegroom, five of them were foolish, and five were wise. The foolish ones, when taking their lamps, brought no oil with them, but the wise brought flasks of oil with their lamps. Since the bridegroom was long delayed, they all became drowsy and fell asleep. At midnight there was a cry, 'behold, the bridegroom! Come out to meet him'

Then all those virgins got up and trimmed their lamps. The foolish ones said to the wise, 'give us some of your oil, for our lamps are going out. But the wise ones replied, 'no, for there may not be enough for us and you. Go instead to the merchants and buy some for yourselves.

While they went off to buy it, the bridegroom came, and those who were ready went into the Weeding feast with him, then the door was locked. Afterwards the other virgins came and said, 'Lord, Lord, open for us! But he said in reply, 'Amen, I say to you I do not know you, 'therefore, stay awake, for you know neither the day nor the hour.

This is the Gospel of the Lord.

All: Praise be to you Lord Jesus Christ.

All please sit.

+A reflection follows from the Scripture readings by the priest/Leader.

INTERCESSIONS:

Leader: (All please stand).

Let us pray with faith and confidence to God our father who lives forever and who can do all things.

As He raised His Son Jesus from the dead, so may He give peace and salvation to both the living and the dead.

1. For the departed friend, brother, sister that he/she may share the light of Christ's resurrection and come into new life and happiness of peace
    We pray O! Lord....................
    Response: Lord hear our prayers.

2. For those whom this World is the be-all and end all,
    That they may come to believe the good news of salvation, renew their Lives and have faith in Christ, who is the way, the truth, and the life.
    We pray O Lord....................
    Response: Lord hear our prayers.

3. For those suffering on account of bereavement that the generosity of their fellow Christians may give them new life and help them to relieve their anxiety.
    We pray O! Lord...........................

4. For all who are gathered here today to pray for our departed friend, brother, sister (name...............) that we may live, and act and speak in the full realization that one day we shall be called upon to answer for our thoughts, words and actions.
    We pray O! Lord....................
    Response: Lord hear our prayers.

CONCLUDING PRAYERS:

Let us pray:

O! Lord, may these humble petitions find favor in your presence for the salvation of our friend, brother, sister (name...............) who have died in Christ, may share everlasting life in heaven, through Jesus Christ our Lord.

Amen.

CONCLUDING HYMN:
GOD BE WITH YOU TILL WE MEET AGAIN.

1. God be with you till we meet again;
   By His counsel guide, up hold you,
   With His sheep in love enfold you;
   God be with you till we meet again.
   Refrain:
   Till we meet again
   Till we meet again
   God be with you
   Till we meet again.

2. God be with you till we meet again!
   'Neath His wings protecting hide you,
   Daily manna still provides you;
   God be with you till we meet again!
   Refrain:

3. God be with you till we meet again!
   When life's perils thick confound you,
   Put His arms unfailing round you;
   God be with you till we meet again
   Refrain:

4. God be with you till we meet again!
   Keeps love's banner floating o'er you,
   Smite death's threatening wave before you;
   God be with you till we meet again!
   Refrain:

PAMPHLET D

FEW MORE LIKELY READINGS IN THE CELEBRATION OF LIFE

FROM THE OLD TESTAMENT:
A READING FROM THE BOOK OF WISDOM,

Chapter 4:7-14.
The just man, though he dies early, shall be at rest.

For the age that is honorable comes not with the passing of time, nor can it be measured in terms of years. Rather, understanding is the hoary crown for men, and an unsullied life, the attainment of old age.

He who pleased god was loved; he who lived among sinners was transported-snatched away, lest wickedness perverts his mind or deceit beguiled his soul; for the witchery of paltry things obscures what is right and the whirl of desire transforms the innocent mind.

Having become perfect in a short while, he reached the fullness of a long career; therefore he sped him out of the midst of wickedness. But the people saw and did not understand, nor did they take this into account.

The word of the Lord.

R). Thanks be to God.

+ A reading from the book of the Ecclesiastes,
Chapter 3:1-8.

There is a giving time for every and a time for every happening under Heavens:

A time for giving birth, a time for dying: a time for planting, a time for uprooting.

A time for killing, a time for healing; a time for knocking down, a time for building.

A time for tears, a time for laughter; a time for mourning, a time for dancing

A time for throwing stones, a time for gathering stones.

A time for embracing, a time to refrain from embracing.

A time for searching, a time for losing;

A time for keeping, a time for throwing away.

A time for tearing, a time for sewing; a time to be silent and a time to speak.

A time for loving, a time for hating; a time for war, a time for peace,

The word of the Lord.

R). Thanks be to God.

+C). A reading from the book of the Prophet Isaiah: Chapter 25:6, 7-9.

On this mountain the Lord of Host will provide for all people.

On the mountain he will destroy the veil that veils all peoples,

The web that is woven over all nations; he will destroy death forever.

The Lord God will wipe away the tears from all faces;

The reproach of his people he will remove from the whole earth;

For the Lord has spoken.

On that day it will be said: "behold our God, to whom we looked to save us!

This is the Lord for whom we Looked; let us rejoice and be glad that he has saved us!"

The word of the Lord. R). Thanks be to God.

And also we the book of Revelation Chapter 12:10-12b.

The book of Isaiah Chapter 61:1-3.

The book of Ezekiel chapter 3:17-21.

And revelation Chapter 21:5-7.

FROM THE NEW TESTAMENT:

+A reading from the first of St. Paul to the Corinthians:

1 Corinthians Chapter 15:51-57.

Brothers and sisters: Behold, I tell you a mystery; we shall not

All fall asleep, but we will all be changed, in an instant in the blink

Of an eye, at the last trumpet.

For the trumpet will sound, the dead will be raised incorruptible, and

We shall be changed. For that which is corruptible must be clothe itself

With incorruptibility, and that which is mortal must clothe itself with immortality. And when this which is corruptible clothes itself with incorruptibility and this which is mortal clothes itself with immortality, then the word that is written shall come about.

Death is swallowed up in victory.

Where, O death is your victory?

Where, O death is your sting?

The sting of death is sin, and the power of sin is the law.

But thanks be to God who gives us the victory through our Lord Jesus Christ.

The word of the Lord.

R). thanks be to God.

+A reading from the letter of St. Paul to the Philippians,
Chapter 3: 20-21.

Brothers and sisters: Our citizenship is in Heaven, and from it

We also await a Savior, the Lord Jesus Christ. He will change

Our lowly body to conform with his glorified Body by the power that enables him also to bring all things into subjection to himself.

The word of the lord.

R). Thanks be to God.

+A reading from the book of Revelation:
Chapter 7:2-4, 9-14.

I John saw another angel come up from the East, holding the seal of the living God. He cried out in a loud voice to the four angels who were given power to damage the land and the sea," Do not damage the land or the sea or the trees until we put the seal on the foreheads of the servant of our God."

I heard the number of those who had been marked with the seal, one hundred and forty four thousand marked from every tribe of the children of Israel.

After this I heard I had a vision of a great multitude, which no one could count, from every nation, race, people, and tongue.

They stood before the throne and before the lamb, wearing white robes and holding palm branches in their hands.

They cried out in a loud voice: "Salvation comes from our God, who is seated on the throne, and from the lamb."

All the angels stood around the throne and around the elders and the four living creatures. They prostrated themselves before the throne, worshiped God, and exclaimed: "Amen, Blessing and glory, wisdom and thanksgiving, honor, power, and mighty be to our God forever and ever. Amen.

Then one of the elders spoke up and said to me, "who are these wearing white robes, and where did they come from?"

I said to him, "My Lord, you are the one who knows."

He said to me, "these are the ones who have survived the time of great distress; they have washed their robes and made them white in the blood of the Lamb.

The Word of the lord.

R). thanks be to God.

+A reading from the book of St. Paul to the Romans:
Chapter 5:5-11.

Brothers and sisters: hope does not disappoint, because the love of God has been poured out into our hearts through the Holy Spirit that has been given to us. For Christ while we were still helpless, died at the appointed Time for the ungodly. Indeed, only with difficulty does one die for the a just person, though perhaps for a good person one might even find courage to die.

But God proves his love for us in that while we were still sinners

Christ died for us. How much more then, since we are now justified by his

Blood, will we be saved through him from the wrath. Indeed, if,

While we were enemies, we were reconciled to God through the death of his son,

How much more, once reconciled, will we be saved by his life?

Not only that, but we also boast of God through our Lord Jesus Christ,

Through whom we have now received reconciliation.

The Word of the Lord.

R). Thanks be to God.

+Reading from the second letter of St. Paul to Timothy:

2nd Timothy Chapter 2:8-13, 3:10-12.

Beloved: remember Jesus Christ, raised from the dead, descendant of

David: such is my Gospel, for which I am suffering, even to the point of

Chain, like a criminal, but the word of God is not chained. Therefore,

I bear with everything for the sake of those who are chosen,

So that they too may obtain the salvation that is in Christ Jesus, together
with eternal glory.

This saying is trustworthy:

If we have died with him

We shall live with him;

If we persevere

We shall also reign with him.

But if we deny him

He will deny us.

If we are unfaithful

He remains faithful,

For he cannot deny himself.

You have followed my teaching, way of life, purpose, faith, patient, love,

Endurance, persecutions, and suffering, such as happened to me in
Antioch, Iconium, and lystra, persecution that I endured.

Yet from all these things the Lord delivered me.

In fact, all who want to live religiously in Christ Jesus will be persecuted.

The Word of the Lord.

R). Thanks be to God.

+A reading from the letter of St. Paul to the Romans: Chapter 14:7-9, 10c-12.

Brothers and sisters, none of us lives for oneself, and no one dies for oneself.

For if we live, we live for the Lord, and if we die, we die for the Lord;

So then, whether we live or die, we are the Lord's.

For this is why Christ died and came to life, that he might be the Lord of both the dead and the living.

Why then do you judge your brother? Or you, why do you look down on your brother?

For we shall all stand before the judgment seat of God; for it is written:

As I live, says the Lord, every knee shall bend before me, and every tongue shall give praise to God.

So then each of us shall give an account of himself to God.

The Word of the Lord.

R). Thanks be to God.

And also: Romans Chapter 8:31b-35, 37-38.

First Corinthians Chapter 15:20-28.

Second Corinthians Chapter 5:1, 6-10.

Hebrew Chapter 10:32-36

James Chapter 1:2-4, 12.

SOME GOSPELS:

+A reading from the Holy Gospel according to St. Luke:

Luke Chapter 7:11-17.

Jesus journeyed to the city called Naim, and his disciples and a large

Crowd accompanied him. As he drew near to the gate of the city, a man who had died was being carried out, the only son of his mother; and she was a widow. A large Crowd from the city was with her when the Lord saw her; he was moved with pity for her and said to her, "do not weep. He stepped forward and touched the coffin; at this the bearers halted, and he said, young man, I tell you, arise!" The dead man sat up and began to speak, and Jesus gave him to his mother. Fear seized them all, and they glorified God, exclaiming, "A great prophet has arisen in our midst," and God has visited his people." This report about him spread through the whole of Judea and in all the surrounding region.

The Holy Gospel of the Lord.

R). Praise to you, Lord Jesus Christ.

+A reading from the Holy Gospel according to St. Luke:

Luke Chapter 11:1-11.

When Mary, the sister of Lazarus, came to where Jesus was and saw Him, she fell at the feet and said to him, "Lord, if you have been here, my Brother would not have died" When Jesus saw her weeping and the Jews who had come with her weeping, he became perturbed and deeply troubled, and said, "where have you laid him.? They said to him, "Sir, come and see." And Jesus wept. So the Jews said, "see how he loved him. But some of them said, "could not the one who opened the eyes of the blind man have done something so that this man would not have died? So Jesus, perturbed again, came to the tomb, it was a cave, and a stone lay across it Jesus said, "take away the stone. "Martha, the dead man's sister, said, to him, Lord by now there will be a stench; he has been dead for four days." Jesus said to her, "Did I not tell you that if you believe you will see the Glory of God?" So they took away the stone. And Jesus raised his eyes and said, "Father, I thank you for hearing me. I know that you always hear me, but because of the Crowd here I have said this, that they may believe that you sent me." And when he has said, he cried out in a loud voice, "Lazarus, come! The dead man came out, tied hand and foot with burial bands, and his face was rapped in a cloth. So Jesus said to them, "untie him and let him go." Now many of the Jews who had come to Mary and seen what he had done began to believe in him.

The Holy Gospel of the Lord.

R). Praise to you, Lord Jesus Christ.

+A reading from the Holy Gospel according to St. John:

John Chapter 6:37 -40.

Jesus said to the Crowd; "Everything that the Father gives me will come to me, and I will not reject anyone who comes to me, because I came down from heaven not to do my own will but the will of the one who sent me. And this is the will of the one who sent me that I should not lose anything of what he gave me, but that I should raise it up on the last day, for this is the will of my father that everyone who sees the Son and believes in him may have eternal life, and I shall raise him up on the last day."

The Gospel of the Lord.

R). Praise to you, Lord Jesus Christ.

+And also Gospel of St. Matthew:
Chapter 5:1-5

St. Mark: Chapter 10:32ff

St. Luke: Chapter 24:13-16, 28-36.

St. John: Chapter 5:25-29.

Chapter 5

SOME LIKELY HYMNS IN THE CELEBRATION OF LIFE

To God be the glory, great things He hath done:

1. To god be the glory, great things He hath done,
   So loved He the world that he gave us His son,
   Who yielded His life our redemption to win,
   And opened the life-gate that all may go in.
   Refrain: Praise the Lord, praise the Lord..........................
   Let the earth hear His voice:
   Praise the Lord, praise the Lord.
   Let the people rejoice;
   Oh, come to the father through Jesus the Son,
   And give Him the glory; great things He Hath done.

2. Oh, perfect redemption, the purchase of blood,
   To every believer the promise of God;
   The vilest offender who truly believe,
   That moment from Jesus a pardon receive.
   Refrain: Praise the Lord,

3. Great things He hath taught us, great things He hath done,
   And great our rejoicing through Jesus the son;
   But purer, and higher, and greater will be
   Our wonder, our transport when Jesus we see.
   Refrain: Praise the Lord.....................

STAND UP STAND UP FOR JESUS:

1. Stand up, stand up for Jesus! Ye soldiers of the cross;
   Lift high His royal banner, it must not suffer loss:
   From victory unto victory, His army shall He lead,
   Till every foe is vanquished, and Christ is Lord indeed.

2. Stand up, stand up for Jesus! The trumpet calls obey:
   Forth to the mighty conflict, in this His glorious day;
   Ye that are men now serve Him against unnumbered foes;
   Let courage rise with danger, and strength to strength oppose.

3. Stand up, stand up for Jesus! Stand in His strength alone,
   The arm of flesh will fail you; ye dare not trust your own;
   Put on the Gospel armor, and watching unto prayer,
   Where calls the voice of duty, be never wanting there.

4. Stand up, stand up for Jesus! The strife will not be long;
   This day the noise of battle, the next the victor's song;
   To Him that overcometh a crown of life shall be;
   He with the King of glory shall reign eternally.

THIS WORLD IS NOT MY HOME:

1. This world is not my home; I'm just a passing through
   My treasures are laid up somewhere beyond the blue;
   The angels beckon me from heaven's open door,
   And I can't feel at home in this world anymore.

Chorus:

O Lord, You know I have no friend like you,
If heaven's not my home, then Lord what will I do?
The angels beckon me from heaven's open door,
And I can't feel at home in this world anymore.

2. They're all expecting me, and that's one thing I know,
   My Savior pardoned me and now I onward go;
   I know He'll take me through though I am and weak and poor,
   And I can't feel at home in this world anymore.

Chorus:

3. I have a loving Savior up in glory land,
   I don't expect to stop until I with Him stand,
   He's waiting now for me in heaven's open door,
   And I can't feel at home in this world anymore.

Chorus:

4. Just up in glory land, we'll live eternally,
   The Saints on every hand are shouting victory,
   Their songs of sweetest praise drift back from heaven's shore,
   And I can't feel at home in this world any more.

Chorus:

IT IS WELL WITH MY SOUL:

1. When peace, like a river, attendeth my way,
   When sorrows like sea billows roll;
   Whatever my lot, Thou hast taught me to say,
   It is well; it is well with my soul.

Refrain:

It is well with my soul,
It is well; it is well with my soul

2. Though Satan should buffet, though trails should come,
   Let this blest assurance control,

That Christ hath regarded my helpless estate,
And hath shed His blood for my soul.

Refrain:

3. My sin-oh, the bliss of this glorious thought!
   My sin, not in part but the whole
   Is nailed to the cross, and I bear it no more,
   Praise the Lord, praise the Lord o my soul.

Refrain:

4. For me, be it Christ, be it Christ hence to live:
   If Jordan above me shall roll,
   No pang shall be mine, for in death as in life
   Thou wilt whisper Thy peace to my soul.

Refrain:

5. But, Lord, "it's for Thee, for thy coming we wait,
   The sky, not the grave, is our goal;
   Oh, trump of the angel! Oh, voice of the Lord!
   Blessed hope, blessed rest of my soul!

Refrain:

6. And Lord, haste the day when the faith shall be sight,
   The clouds be rolled back as a scroll;
   The trump shall resound, and the Lord shall descend,
   Even so, it is well with my soul.

Refrain:

WHAT A FRIEND WE HAVE IN JESUS:

What a friend we have in Jesus,
All our sins and grief to bear!
What a privilege to carry
Everything to God in prayer!
O what peace we often forfeit,
O what needless pain we bear,
All because we do not carry
Everything to God in prayer!
Have we trials and temptations?
Is there a trouble anywhere?
We should never be discouraged,
Take it to the Lord in prayer,
Can we find a friend so faithful?
Who will all our sorrows share?
Jesus knows our every weakness,
Take it to the Lord in prayer.
Are we weak and heavy-laden?
Cumbered with a load of care
Precious Savior, still our refuge.......
Take it to the lord in prayer,
In His arms He'll take and shield thee,
Thou wilt find a solace there.

I NEED THEE EVERY HOUR:

I need Thee every hour,
Most gracious Lord;
No tender voice like Thine
Can peace afford?
I need Thee, oh, I need Thee;
Every hour I need Thee;
Oh, bless me now, my savior!

I come to Thee.
I need Thee every hour,
Stay thou nearby,
Temptation lose their power
When Thou art nigh.
I need Thee every hour,
In joy or pain,
Come quickly and abide
Or life is vain.
I need Thee every hour,
Teach me Thy will;
And Thy rich promises
In me fulfill.
I need Thee every hour,
Most holy One,
Oh, make me Thine indeed,
Thou blessed Son.

O LORD MY GOD WHEN I IN AWESOME WONDER:

O Lord my God!
When I in awesome wonder
Consider all the works
Thy hands have made,
I see the stars,
I hear the rolling thunder,
The power throughout
The universal displayed;

Refrain:

Then sings my soul,
My savior God to Thee,
How great Thou art,

How great Thou art!
Then sings my soul,
My savior God, to Thee
How great Thou art,
How great Thou art!

Refrain:

When through the woods
and forest glades I wander
and hear the birds
sing sweetly in the trees;
When I look down
from lofty mountain grandeur,
and hear the brook,
and feel the gentle breeze;

Refrain:

And when I think
that God His Son not sparing,
sent Him to die...........
I scarce can take it in,
that on the cross
my burden gladly bearing,
He bled and died to take away my sin;

Refrain:

Chapter 6

SOME MORE GOOD RESPONSORIAL PSALMS

PSALM 25:6 AND 7B, 17-18, AND 20-21.

Response: 1. To you, O Lord, I lift my soul.

Or

1. No one who waits for you, O Lord, will ever be put to shame.

Remember that your compassion, O Lord, and your kindness are from of old. In your kindness remember me, Because of your goodness, O Lord.

Response...................

Relieve the troubles of my heart, and bring me out of my distress,

Put an end to my affliction and my suffering; and take away all my sins.

Response...................

Preserve my life, and rescue me, let integrity and uprightness preserve me

Because I wait for you, O Lord.

Response...

PSALM 27:1, 4, 7, AND 8B AND 9A, 13-14.

Response: 1. The Lord is my light and my salvation.

Or

2. I believe that I shall see the good things of the Lord in the Land of the living.

The Lord is my light and my salvation;

Whom shall I fear?

The Lord is my life's refuge;

Of whom should I be afraid?

Response.................

One thing I ask of the Lord;

This I seek to dwell in the house of the Lord,

All the days of my life,

That I may gaze on the loveliness of the Lord, and contemplate his temple.

Response...

Hear, O Lord, the sound of my call;

Have pity on me and answer me,

Your presence, O Lord, I seek.

Hide not your face from me.

Response...

PSALM 51: 12-13, 14-15, 18-19.

Response: I WILL POUR CLEAN WATER ON YOU AND WASH AWAY ALL YOUR SINS:

A clean heart creates for me, O God, and a steadfast Spirit renew within me, cast me not out from your presence, and your Holy Spirit take not from me.

Response...

Give me back the joy of your salvation, and a willing spirit sustain in me,

I will teach transgressors your ways, and sinners shall return to you.

Response...

For you are not pleased with sacrifice;

Should I offer a burnt offering, you would not accept it,

My sacrifice, O God, is a contrite spirit;

A heart contrite and humbled, O God, you will not spurn.

Response...

PSALM 88:2-3, 4-6, 7-8.

Response: LET MY PRAYERS COME BEFORE YOU, LORD.

O Lord, my God, by day I cry out;

At night I clamor in your presence,

Let my prayers come before you;

Incline your ear to my call for help.

Response...

For my soul is surfeited with troubles

And my life draws near to the nether world,

I am numbered with those who go down into the pit;

I am a man without strength.

Response...

PSALM 90:3-4, 5-6, 12-13, 14 and 17.

Response: —

IN EVERY AGE, O LORD, YOU HAVE BEEN OUR REFUGE.

You turn man back to dust,

Saying, "Return, O children of men."

For a thousand years in your sight

Are as yesterday, now that it is past, or as a watch of the night.

Response...

You make an end of them in their sleep;

The next morning they are like the changing grass,

Which at dawn spring up anew?

But by evening wilts and fades.

Response...

Teach us to number our days aright,

That we may gain wisdom of heart.

Return, O Lord! How long?

Have pity on your servant!

Response...

Fill us at daybreak with kindness,

That we may shout for joy and gladness all our days.

And may the gracious care of the Lord our God be ours,

Prosper the work of our hands for us!

Prosper the work of our hands!

Response...

A LITTLE PERSONAL PROFILE OF REV. FR. DR. ALPHONSUS EMESHIOBI OBIKA-OSUOHA.

PERSONAL: Rev. Fr. Dr. Alphonsus. E.O.O. is the youngest of the four siblings of Chief and Mrs. Obika Osuoha of their blessed memories, from Ubahaeze, Orodo in Mbaitoli LGA, in IMO State of Nigeria.

Rev. Fr. Obi lost both parents at a very early age and was raised by his grand-mother Mrs. Hannah Enyidiya Okorie (of blessed memory) who showed him with so much love that he never realized she was not his biological mother until he became an adult. His maternal families were very religious and well organized. He learned the values of hard work, the need for a good education, and respect for humanity. Consequently, he challenged himself to become successful in whatever thing he laid his hands on.

Even though, he grew up in an Anglican environment (his maternal home), he had great passion to serve God in whatever capacity He wanted him to do. While some of his mates talked of becoming Doctors, Lawyers, Engineers, etc. He developed high admiration for Roman Catholic Priest and had an ardent desire to become one. This burning desire led him to the vocation to the Priesthood, in line with his paternal Catholic faith.

EDUCATION: Rev. Fr. Obi attended St. Lazarus Catholic Primary School, Orodo in Mbaitoli L.G.A; where he obtained his First School Leaving Certificate. He gained admission into St. Mary's Minor Seminary at Umuowa in Orlu, Imo State. After the preparatory seminary, he proceeded to St. Peter Claver's Seminary, Okpuala, where he was until the unfortunate Nigeria-Biafra civil war broke out. After the war in 1970, Fr. Obi decided not to go back to the Seminary but rather, attended New Bethel College Onitsha, DMGS Onitsha to pursue secular life. After his graduation, the vocation to the Priesthood once more became an obsession to him. He gained admission to Bigard Memorial Major Seminary, Enugu and SS Peter and Paul Bodija Major Seminary, Ibadan (an affiliate of Urban University Rome). Fr. Alphonsus preferred going to Bigard Memorial Seminary Enugu, which was closer to his home. After staying only but two weeks in Bigard, he changed his mind and left for Bodija Seminary Ibadan, where he studied Philosophy and Theology for good seven years. Life in Bodija was very tough and uncertain as he witnessed only 12 men out of the 176 Seminarians that he started with, made it to the Priesthood. Fr. Obi graduated with BD (Bachelor of Divinity), and in December 1981, he was ordained a Deacon. Thereafter in February 14th, 1982, he was one of the 92 providential young men who were ordained a Priest by late

His Holiness, St. Pope John Paul II of his blessed memory in Kaduna, on his first trip to Nigeria. Rev. Fr. Obi was at the moment ordained a diocesan Priest for Lagos Archdiocese, and then posted to Lagos after his ordination to his Priesthood. He became the first indigenous Priest from Orodo, a position that attracted an admiration from the entire community, irrespective of one's religious affiliation.

PRIESTHOOD EXPERIENCE: Rev. Fr. Dr. Obi's first assignment was at the Catholic Church in Badagry as an Associate Priest. After six months, he became the Pastor in charge of Immaculate Conception Catholic Church, Adodo in Ogun State. In 1983, he was transferred to St. Mary's Catholic Church Ilaro also in Ogun State, where he started learning and speaking the native Yoruba language of the people and conducted Masses in that language. He built a parsonage with a basement and renovated Churches in most of the towns in his Parish.

In 1985, Rev. Fr. Dr. Obi received a scholarship from the Opus Dei (the work God) Society, a religious Order made up of Priests, Rev. Brothers, the religious and laymen from Lagos Archdiocese and Rome to study at the (Centro Academico Romano Della Santa Croce) i.e. Central University of Academics of the Holy Cross, where he obtained his Doctorate degree in Theology. He further studied Canon Law (Church Law, and obtained the licentiate (License). Rev. Fr. Dr. Obi came back from Rome to the Archdiocese of Lagos and served as Parish Priest first at SS Mulumba and David Ikate Lawanson, Surulere Lagos from 1989 to 1996, where he erected St. Ann's Catholic Church building and a parsonage at Itire, Lawanson. He also started a building that would replace the central Parish church building before he left the place. The same year in 1996, he was transferred to St. Augustine's Catholic Church, Ikorodu, Lagos, which has nine outstations. By then, Rev. Fr. Dr. Obi erected many Church buildings in some of these outstations that had none before.

THE JOURNEY TO UNITED STATES OF AMERICA: While in Ikorodu in 1998, Fr. Obi was visited by a gang of 21 armed robbers in the night. Not knowing their strengths initially, Fr. Obi started firing his gun at them. The robbers besieged his parsonage by that late hour of 1.00am to 4.00am. They robbed all his valuable possessions without any intervention from the Police force. They threatened and swore to kill him if he refused to open the door. Fr. Obi escaped death by hiding himself in the ceiling when they entered the parsonage. They ransacked the whole rooms and even directed their bullets at every corner of the house. After this incident, Fr. Obi became traumatized, shocked, phobic, agitated, and unable to trust anybody anymore. He was transferred to a new Parish but the place was still within the reach of the invading armed robbers. This did not mitigate his situation. The best option, as suggested by his therapeutic Doctor was for him to leave the country for some time. His Archbishop granted him the permission and Rev. Fr. Dr. Obi came to the United States of America, where he is still recovering from the ugly experience. Since then, Fr. Obi has been struggling for his dear life, trying to make ends meet. He conducts Holy Masses whenever he is called. He also counsels troubled families, substance abuse (drugs and alcohol) recoveries, and business advisory.

JESUS, I trust in YOU

Printed in the United States
by Baker & Taylor Publisher Services

Printed in the United States
by Baker & Taylor Publisher Services